W9-DBR-289

MILITARY UNIFORMS & WEAPONRY
-THE POSTER BOOK OF-
World War II

Copyright © 1987 New Orchard Editions Ltd.
All rights reserved.

This 1987 edition
published by Military Press
distributed by Crown Publishers, Inc.,
225 Park Avenue South,
New York, New York 10003

All rights reserved. No part of this book may be
reproduced or transmitted in any form or by any
means, electronic or mechanical, including
photocopying, recording, or by any information
storage and retrieval system, without permission in
writing from the publisher.

Created by David Graves
Designed by Crispin Goodall

ISBN 0-517-64472-X

Printed in Italy

MILITARY UNIFORMS & WEAPONRY
-THE POSTER BOOK OF-
World War II

90 Authentic Figures in Color   Illustrated by Malcolm McGregor
INTRODUCTION BY ANDREW MOLLO

MILITARY PRESS
NEW YORK

INTRODUCTION

The end of World War 1 saw the emergence of many independent states as the vanquished monarchies found themselves in the throes of major social and political upheaval.

The greatest territorial changes had taken place in Eastern Europe, where Russia, defeated and in the midst of civil war, was being stripped of its empire. The republics to emerge from former Russian territory were Poland, Estonia, Latvia, Lithuania and Finland. The republics of Czechoslovakia and Hungary were established in countries formerly part of the Austro-Hungarian Hapsburg empire. The Kingdom of Yugoslavia unified Serbs, Montenegrins, Bosnians, Slovenes and Macedonians under a Serbian monarch. Rumania and Bulgaria retained their dynasties.

While the victors demobilised and tried to convince themselves that the 'great' war had been the war to end all wars, the newly independent nations set about building armies, to ensure their independence. The cadre for these new armies had spent much of their life in the service of the Austrian Emperor or Russian Tsar, and were happy to continue in this tradition. But for nationalistic and political reasons a complete break with the past was called for, and attempts were made to create 'new' armies with new uniforms, which would mirror the political aspirations of the country.

It was natural that it should be to the victorious nations that these emerging armies looked for advice and equipment, and most turned to France. Politically and culturally France had influenced Eastern Europe to such an extent that in some countries French had become a second language. In the 1920s France could claim to have invented military science as it was then known, and her victory over Germany had confirmed the prestige of her arms.

While France provided the model for soldiers' uniforms, and Belgian, Italian, Polish, Soviet and Yugoslav armies wore the French 'Adrian' steel helmet, England set the trend for officers. The English popularised the shirt-and-tie uniform, the long-skirted tunic with huge patch pockets and the flat-topped and horizontal-peaked service cap. So closely did Belgian, Greek and Rumanian officers copy this style of dress that it is often difficult to tell them all apart. The English steel helmet was worn by the armies of Greece, Norway, Portugal and the United States of America.

The Red Army also had reasons to make a break with tradition and, after a determined effort to go French in the 1920s, reverted step by step to its traditional uniforms. Not one of the former Russian territories adopted Russian-style uniforms. Poland developed its own distinct uniforms and re-introduced many traditional features such as the *czapka* and zigzag lace which were so reminiscent of the Napoleonic wars.

The countries which had formed part of the Austro-Hungarian Empire such as Czechoslovakia dressed their armies in khaki with an English-style peaked cap for officers and a rather Germanic uniform for other ranks. Hungarian uniform continued in the Austrian tradition. By the outbreak of war military uniform can be divided into the following distinct groups. The Anglo-Saxon countries together with their colonies and dominions were developing 'colonial' uniforms which had been developed for unconventional warfare in varied climates. European uniform was more conventional and on the whole followed the French lead, with certain concessions to English fashion. Russia continued its own line of development. In the Far East both Japan and China had adapted European uniform to suit their own industrial capabilities and climatic conditions.

Soon after the beginning of the war many of the smaller armies had been swept from the board, and military uniform polarised around England, Germany, Soviet Russia and Japan. The personnel of the defeated armies who managed to escape to England or the Middle East were issued with British uniforms and equipment. They attempted all the same to preserve their national identity by wearing as much of their old insignia on battle dress as they could, and designing new formation flashes to conform with British practice. Once America entered the war she took some of the strain off England's over-stretched resources by supplying the largest exile force, the Free French, with U.S. clothing and equipment.

In the east, Germany's satellites, unprepared and ill-equipped for a long drawn out war of attrition, came to rely more and more on German *matériel*. This inevitably led to an increased German influence in the appearance of Hungarian, Rumanian and Slovakian troops and even of the 'Tsarist' Bulgarians.

Russia was completely oblivious to new trends in modern military clothing and equipment, partly because of her limited industrial capacity, but partly also because she had found by experience that traditional Russian peasant-style uniform and the most rudimentary equipment was not only the cheapest, but also the most practical, for the climate and conditions in which the army had to fight.

Soviet Russia also equipped exiled Polish, Czech and Yugoslav formations with Soviet uniforms.

To this day the basic Soviet uniform is a greatcoat, shirt, breeches and high leather boots, and any recent departure has been brought about by Russia's new stance as a power capable of mounting airborne and amphibious operations anywhere in the world.

There is no doubt that at the beginning of the war Germany led in the field of uniform technology, and had pioneered a number of special uniforms which were to provide models for other nations. But once war was declared she contributed little to the development of new clothing or manufacturing techniques. Any innovations she did introduce in the field of synthetic textiles were due primarily to her deteriorating raw material situation.

The concept of one basic uniform which was both practical in the field and smart enough to enhance morale and wear as a full dress or for walking out, lasted until the advent of mechanisation. Mechanisation was to start a trend which began with the mechanic's overall, and ended with two distinct types of uniform – combat dress and service dress – neither of which had anything in common. The overall was an absolute necessity for any soldier forced to work with large pieces of oily machinery such as tanks. In fact all the armies who participated in World War 2 introduced either one- or two-piece overalls for the tank crews. Germany designed a special black tank uniform in 1935, but also began to issue overalls during the war for economy reasons. The gap widened with the advent of airborne troops who had to be supplied with special clothing which could hardly be worn off duty. Once again Russia, the first to experiment effectively with parachute troops, turned to the overall. The Germans were quick to realise the importance of this new arm, and tried out a complete dress which could be safely worn during a fall, and in action on the ground. This included a special rimless steel helmet, a smock to wear over the personal equipment during the jump, trousers and special boots with rubber soles. After Germany's successful airborne operations at the beginning of the war, England formed her own parachute troops, and dressed them in a copy of the German uniform. America also at first issued its parachutists with a flying helmet, overall and lace-up ankle boots, but by the time she committed them to action she had modified the normal combat uniform, but unlike the British and Germans, the Americans found that the smock which covered the equipment for the jump was not necessary and even delayed the combat readiness of a paratrooper on landing. Instead every item of equipment which could possibly get entangled with the parachute lines was strapped carefully to the body with lengths of webbing strap.

Both airborne and armoured troops considered themselves an élite and tended to wear their special clothing off duty. In the German army the black tank uniform was issued in addition to the field-grey clothing, for wear when on duty with the vehicle, but was so proudly worn on all occasions that the second set of field-grey clothing was no longer issued during the war.

England's great contribution to world uniform was the development of the colour khaki, and the 'battle dress' which she first introduced in 1937. Few people seem to have anything good to say about 'B.D.', and it was very difficult to look smart in it, and yet it so impressed the Americans that they began to issue it in 1944. In the same year Germany copied it because of its simplicity to manufacture and economic use of cloth. After the war British battle dress was adopted by many countries, and although discarded by the English and Americans, is still in extensive use in other armies.

America was the first to begin to separate the service and field uniforms by introducing a field jacket in 1941. In 1943 after extensive trials, she revolutionised the design of combat clothing with the introduction of a lightweight weatherproof uniform, which could be adapted to varying climatic conditions by the addition of layers of various kinds of undergarments. This layer principle is today utilised throughout the world.

1 Germany: Private 138th Mountain Rifle Regiment, Trondheim 1940

Personnel in mountain units wore standard infantry field uniform with ski cap, baggy climbing trousers, climbing boots with studded soles, and short elasticated puttees. The arm colour was bright green while a further distinguishing mark was the edelweiss in white metal on the left side of the ski cap, and in white on a dark green oval ground on the upper right sleeve.

Equipment: Standard infantry equipment with rucksack instead of the pack and a larger-capacity water bottle.

Weapons: German Mauser Gew. 98k with an additional butt plate to prevent the wooden butt from being damaged by the cleats on the sides of the soles of mountain boots.

2 Germany: Infantry General Eduard Dietl, Narvik 1940

The popular commander of the 3rd Mountain Division and Narvik Group won his Knight's Cross in May 1940, and Oak Leaves two months later. He wears the ski cap and old-style piped field blouse. On his right breast is the enamelled badge for Army Mountain Guides.

3 Germany: Private 159th Infantry Regiment, Norway 1940

Both the Germans and the Allies suffered severely from exposure and were forced to improvise winter clothing from whatever was available – even captured enemy uniforms.

Equipment: Machine-gunners wore standard infantry equipment, but insteadof two ammunition pouches they carried a pistol and a leather case containing machine-gun stripping and cleaning tools and an anti-aircraft sight.

Weapons: German MG.34 light machine-gun, 08 or P.38 service pistols and stick grenade 24.

1 *German mountain trooper*   2 *German general*   3 *German infantryman*

4 *German tank officer*   5 *German general*   6 *German infantryman*

4 Germany: 2nd Lieutenant 1st Tank Regiment, France 1940
The black uniform was originally introduced for wear when actually on duty with the vehicle, and with all other orders of dress the field-grey uniform with pink *Waffenfarbe* was worn. The beret incorporated a padded crash helmet.

Equipment: Normally only a waistbelt and pistol holster were worn on the person, while all other kit was stowed away in the tank.

Weapons: German M.08 Parabellum (Luger) or Walther P.38 service pistols.

5 Germany: General of infantry, 1940
Generals were distinguished by gold cords and piping on the cap, gold-embroidered red collar patches, gold and silver braid shoulder straps and red *Lampassen* on the breeches or trousers. Cap badges remained silver until January 1943, when they too became gold.

Equipment: Regulation waistbelt with gilt metal two-pronged belt buckle.

Weapons: General officers normally wore a small-calibre automatic pistol.

6 Germany: Lance-corporal 10th Panzer Grenadier Regiment, France 1940
Panzer Grenadiers tended to fight lighter-equipped than infantry because their kit was carried in armoured personnel carriers or lorries.

Equipment: Standard infantry equipment with the anti-gas cape in the pouch on the chest.

Weapons: German Gew. 98k service rifle and stick grenade 24.

7 Germany: Private of artillery, France 1940

Mounted personnel were issued with breeches and riding boots in place of long trousers and marching boots. Arm-of-service colour was red.

Equipment: Mounted personnel were not issued with packs because they carried their kit in saddle bags. The straps supporting are the cavalry pattern.

Weapons: German Mauser 98k rifle.

8 Germany: Lance-corporal Assault Company Koch, Eben Emael 1940

The olive-green cotton duck one-piece jump smock was worn over the equipment; on landing it was removed and replaced under the equipment.

Equipment: Standard infantry equipment was modified so as not to cause injury to the wearer on landing. Ammunition and flare cartridges were carried in cloth bandoliers, and the gas mask was removed from its metal cannister and carried in a soft cloth bag.

Weapons: German Mauser 98k rifle.

Germany: Private 18th Motorised Engineer Battalion, Northern France 1940

Engineers wore standard field service uniform with black *Waffenfarbe*. This engineer wears stone-grey trousers, which began to be replaced by field-grey ones in 1940.

Equipment: Special technical equipment and apparatus was issued for a particular operation, and could include heavy-duty wire cutters and smoke cannisters.

Weapons: German Mauser 98k service rifle.

7 *German artilleryman*   8 *German paratrooper*   9 *German engineer*

10 *Belgian mountain trooper*   11 *Belgian general*   12 *Belgian motorcyclist*

10 Belgium: Corporal 2nd Regiment of Ardennes Rifles, Belgium 1940
The shortened greatcoat and leather leggings were worn instead of standard infantry greatcoat and puttees. Regimental distinctions were the green beret and boar's head badge.

Equipment: Standard Belgian infantry equipment with German-pattern ammunition pouches.

Weapons: Belgian M.1889 7·65 mm. service rifle.

11 Belgium: Leopold III King of the Belgians, Belgium 1940
As C.-in-C. Belgian Army he wears the uniform of a general. This English-style service dress was common to all army officers.

Equipment: Regulation officer's waistbelt and cross-strap.

12 Belgium: Motorcyclist, Belgium 1940
This brown leather uniform was also worn by crews of armoured vehicles, who also wore the French armoured troop helmet. Motorcyclists and motorised troops wore the special leather-covered helmet illustrated.

13 Great Britain: Private 2nd Battalion Seaforth Highlanders, France 1940

This highlander wears the 1937-pattern battle dress with fly front and concealed buttons under the pocket flaps. The Camerons formed part of the 51st Highland Division whose formation sign is shown.

Equipment: Pattern 1937 web equipment with gas mask worn on the chest.

Weapons: British rifle No. 4 Mark I (better known as the SMLE or ·303).

14 Great Britain: Lance-corporal infantry, 1940

This was the standard uniform of the British army at the beginning of the war, and it remained virtually unchanged throughout.

Equipment: Pattern 1937 web equipment with gas mask slung over the shoulder. The basic pouches were designed to carry two Bren magazines, a number of grenades or small arms ammunition.

Weapons: British rifle No. 3 Mark I.

15 France: Motorcyclist of Motorised Dragoons (Dragons portés), 1940

Motorised Dragoon regiments included squadrons of motorcyclists and infantry transported in half-tracks. The regulation uniform for motorcyclists was the helmet shown and either a brown leather single breasted coat, or a rubberised coat with matching trousers.

Equipment: Regulation French infantry equipment.

Weapons: French rifle (Fusil) 1907–15.

13 *Scottish highlander* 14 *British infantryman* 15 *French infantryman*

16 *British guards officer*   17 *British general*   18 *British guardsman*

16 Great Britain: Captain Willie Forbes 3rd Battalion Coldstream Guards, Libya December 1940
Even during the battle of Sidi Barani guards officers managed to establish and maintain their own distinctive style of dress. This battalion was also responsible for popularisng full-length Hebron sheepskin coats. The helmet is covered with sacking to soften its outline and blend it with its surroundings.

Equipment: Pattern 1937 web equipment basic set for officers, with binocular case on the right. In his hand he carries the officer's haversack.

Weapons: British Webley ·455 Mark VI Pistol No. 1.

17 Great Britain: General Sir Archibald Wavell, Libya 1940
By desert standards Wavell was very correctly dressed with British warm, breeches and field boots. He makes an interesting comparison with Monty.

18 Great Britain: Guardsman, Libya 1940
Guardsmen continued to wear the stiff service dress cap in the desert. The rest of the uniform consisting of khaki drill shirt, shorts and khaki woollen pullover was standard issue.

Equipment: Pattern 1937 web equipment with gas mask on the chest, and small pack on the back and water bottle on the right hip.

Weapons: British rifle No. 1 Mark III.

19 Italy: Lieutenant Scalise, Commander Assault Gun Battery 132nd Ariete Armoured Division, North Africa 1940–1
The three-quarter-length double-breasted leather coat and blocked leather helmet with padded rim and neck flap were standard issue for crews of armoured vehicles. Rank badges were normally worn on the left breast.

Equipment: Regulation officer's waistbelt and binoculars.

Weapons: Italian Beretta 1934 9 mm. automatic pistol.

20 Italy: Marshal of Italy Badoglio, Libya 1940
This lightweight service dress was standard for all officers and was usually made of gabardine. The five-pointed star on the collar was the former emblem of the Italian army, and was common to all ranks in all arms.

Equipment: Regulation officer's waistbelt and cross-strap.

21 Italy: Captain 70th Infantry Regiment (Sirte Division), Libya 1940
Normally each division had two infantry regiments and an artillery regiment, each of which was identified by coloured collar patches. The divisional sign in the form of a metal or cloth shield was worn on the upper left sleeve.

Equipment: Regulation officer's waistbelt and cross-strap.

Weapons: Italian Beretta 1934 9 mm. automatic pistol.

19 *Italian tank officer*   20 *Italian marshal*   21 *Italian infantry officer*

22 German mountain trooper   23 German SS infantryman   24 German paratroop officer

22 Germany: Corporal 143 Mountain Rifle Regiment, Greece April 1941

Arm-of-service colour was grass-green, and mountain troops were further distinguished by a white metal edelweiss on the left side of the cap, and an oval dark green cloth badge with the edelweiss in white, which was worn on the upper right sleeve.

Equipment: Standard mountain troop equipment.

Weapons German MP.40 sub-machine-gun.

23 Germany: Lance-corporal SS Motorised Bodyguard Regiment Adolf Hitler, Greece 1941

The collar of the field blouse, which was worn under the camouflage smock, was left exposed to display rank badges.

Equipment: Standard infantry equipment with map case.

Weapons: German Mauser 98k rifle.

24 Germany: Air-force 2nd Lieutenant 1st Parachute Rifle Regiment, Crete 1941

Parachute troops were distinguished by yellow *Waffenfarbe*, which appeared on the collar patches and shoulder straps. Members of the 1st and 2nd Parachute Rifle Regiments and the Parachute Division wore a green cuffband on the right cuff. The German parachutist's landing position necessitated the use of knee pads.

Equipment: Air-force officer's belt, holster and map case, and issue straps supporting.

25 Australia: Corporal 6th Infantry Division, Greece 1941

The Australian battle dress still included the tunic of World War I vintage. The slouch hat was worn with the flap down or folded up in which case it was fastened with either the regimental or Australian badge.

Equipment: Pattern 1908 web equipment.

Weapons: British rifle No. 1 Mark III.

26 Greece: Corporal of rifles (Evzones), Greece 1941

This shows the *Evzone* version of the Greek army field uniform. The standard version consisted of a tunic and pantaloons, which were worn with ankle boots and puttees.

Equipment: Natural-coloured leather equipment, with olive-green canvas haversack and pack.

Weapons: French rifle (*fusil*) 1907–15.

27 Yugoslavia: Private of infantry, Yugoslavia 1941

Although the standard uniform of the Yugoslav army was this greyish khaki, World War I Serbian uniforms were also in general use. The steel helmet was the French model with the Yugoslav coat of arms on the front.

Equipment: Standard brown leather Yugoslav infantry equipment.

Weapons: Yugoslav M.1924 7·92 mm. service rifle.

25 *Australian infantryman*   26 *Greek rifleman*   27 *Yugoslav infantryman*

28 *British tank man*   29 *French légionnaire*   30 *Indian infantryman*

28 Great Britain: Corporal Royal Tank Regiment, North Africa 1941
The black beret with its silver badge distinguished men of the Royal Tank Regiment from other personnel. Goggles were an absolute necessity in the desert.

Equipment: Pattern 1937 web equipment set for Royal Armoured Corps and Royal Signals personnel employed with those units.

Weapons: British 0·38 in. service revolver.

29 France: Private French Foreign legion in the 1st Free French Brigade, Bir Hakiem 1941
This bearded pioneer wears British K.D. shirt and shorts and webbing anklets together with the famous white kepi.

Equipment: Regulation French infantry equipment.

Weapons: French MAS 1936 rifle.

30 India: Private of infantry 4th Indian Division, North Africa 1941
The Indian army pioneered the use of knitted pullovers, while the rest of the uniform followed closely the British pattern. The very long and wide shorts, known to the British as 'Bombay bloomers', were also typical of Indian uniform. The hessian helmet cover was gathered and hung down at the back of the neck as on a *puggree* and was used to cover the face in dust and sand storms.

Equipment: Pattern 1908 web equipment.

Weapons: British rifle No. 1 Mark I.

31 Germany: Private 2nd Machine-gun Battalion (15th Pz. Div.), North Africa 1941

This rather Anglified tropical uniform was worn by German troops on arrival in North Africa, but after practical experience a more practical and comfortable uniform was evolved.

Equipment: Standard German infantry equipment made of olive-green webbing and light brown leatherwork.

Weapons: German Mauser 98k rifle.

32 Germany: Major-General von Ravenstein, Commander 21st Armoured Division, North Africa November 1941

There was no special tropical dress for general officers, and they normally wore issue uniforms with their appropriate badges of rank.

Equipment: Regulation general officer's waistbelt.

Weapons: German Walther 7·65 mm. automatic pistol.

33 Germany: Corporal 5th Tank Regiment in the 5th Light Division (later 21st Armoured Division), North Africa 1941

Tank troops, retained, out of pride on their arm, the death's heads from their black tunics, and wore them on the lapels of their tropical tunics. Crews of armoured vehicles received the side cap instead of the field cap, because the large peak of the latter was inconvenient inside an armoured vehicle.

Equipment: Regulation tropical version of the other ranks' waist-belt.

Weapons: German 08 or P.38 service pistol.

31 *German infantryman* 32 *German general* 33 *German tank man*

34 *Italian infantryman*   35 *Italian general*   36 *Italian colonial infantryman*

34 Italy: Corporal Young Fascist Armoured Division, North Africa 1942
This army division was recruited from young fascists and wore army tropical clothing with black tasselled fez and rank chevrons.

Equipment: Standard Italian infantry equipment.

Weapons: Mannlicher-Carcano M.1938 7·35 mm. rifle.

35 Italy: Brigadier Bignani, Second-in-Command Trento Division, North Africa September 1942
He wears the tropical bush jacket or *sabariana* and the tropical version of the field cap with matching peak and flap. German officers found the *sabariana* a comfortable garment and wore it on a number of occasions.

Equipment: Regulation officer's wasitbelt and cross-strap.

Weapons: Italian 1934 9 mm. Beretta automatic pistol.

36 Italy: Lance-corporal (Muntaz) 3rd Libyan Battalion, North Africa 1942
Like the colonial troops of England and France, Italian *Askaris* wore a combination of Italian uniform and native dress. Each battalion was identified by a different colour tarbush and sash. The chevron denoted his rank, and the two white stars, six years' service.

Equipment: Standard Italian infantry equipment.

Weapons: Italian Mannlicher-Carcano M.91 TS carbine.

37 Germany: General Staff Major, northern sector Russian front 1941
General staff officers wore specially-embroidered *Litzen* on their collar patches and crimson stripes on their breeches.

Equipment: Regulation officer's waistbelt, service binoculars and issue pocket lamp.

38 Germany: Corporal Military Police (Feldgendarmerie), northern sector Russian front 1941
Apart from the gorget with luminous inscription, military policemen were further identified by the orange police badge on the upper left sleeve of the tunic and a brown cuff-band with grey inscription 'Feldgendarmerie' on the lower left sleeve of both the tunic and great-coat. The coat was made of a rubberised fabric and was issued to motorcyclists and pillion passengers.

39 Finland: Private of infantry, northern sector 1941
This infantryman wears the light-weight summer version of the M.1936 field service uniform. The steel helmet was the 1935 German model.

Equipment: Finnish equipment closely followed the German pattern.

Weapons: Finnish 7·62 mm. M.39 service rifle.

37 *German staff officer*   38 *German military policeman*   39 *Finnish infantryman*

40 *German SS infantryman*   41 *Italian cavalry officer*   42 *German infantry officer*

40 Germany: Private 2nd Battalion SS Infantry Regiment Deutschland, centre sector Russian front 1941

This machine-gunner wears the standard SS camouflaged 'tiger jacket' and steel helmet cover with summer pattern exposed.

Equipment: Machine-gunner's version of the standard German infantry equipment.

Weapons: German Walther P.38 service pistol and German Mg.34 light machine-gun.

41 Italy: Captain Corinaldi, 3rd Savoy Cavalry Regiment, southern sector Russian front 1941

This is the regulation officer's service dress with the M.1935 steel helmet. The first four cavalry regiments all had the black cross on the steel helmet. The red tie was this regiment's distinction in commemoration of the Battle of Madonnadi Campana in 1706, whereas the black cross on the helmet was worn by the first four cavalry regiments.

Equipment: Regulation officer's waistbelt and cross-strap.

Weapons: Cavalry officer's sabre and Italian Beretta 9 mm. 1834 automatic pistol.

42 Germany: Captain of infantry, centre sector Russian front 1941

As the war progressed it was more typical for officers to wear issue uniforms in the field.

Equipment: Regulation officer's waistbelt.

Weapons: German 08 automatic pistol.

43 U.S.S.R.: Junior Politruk (Lieutenant) of infantry, 1941
Political commissars (*Komissars* or *Politruks*) wore the same uniform as their active counterparts, but were not entitled to gold edging to the collar patches or sleeve chevrons. A further badge of distinction was a red cloth five-pointed star on the lower left sleeve.

Equipment: Regulation officer's waistbelt and cross-strap.

44 U.S.S.R.: Army general, 1941
The single-breasted 'French' was introduced in 1935, and generals' rank titles in 1940. The three lowest general officer ranks did not wear red collar patches but those in the colour of their arm-of-service.

45 U.S.S.R.: Lieutenant of artillery, 1941
The side cap or *pilotka* was generally authorised for all ranks in 1935. The officer's side cap and shirt was piped in the arm-of-service colour whereas those of their men were not.

Equipment: Regulation officer's waistbelt.

43 *Russian political commissar*   44 *Russian general*   45 *Russian artillery officer*

46 *Russian tank man*   47 *Russian infantryman*   48 *Russian NKVD officer*

46 U.S.S.R.: Corporal of tank troops, 1941

A khaki one-piece overall replaced the black one at the beginning of the war and remained in use until the end. It was usually worn over the shirt and left unbuttoned at the throat so that the collar patches on the shirt collar were visible. Sometimes collar patches, and later shoulder boards, were worn on the overall.

47 U.S.S.R.: Sergeant of infantry, 1941

N.C.O.s' ranks and badges were re-introduced in 1940, and in this particular case the striped collar patch and brass triangle indicated the rank, while the colour of the stripes and the brass collar badge identified the man as an infantryman. The steel helmet still retains the comb of its French predecessor from which it was evolved. In 1940 it began to be replaced by a simpler new model.

Equipment: Brown leather ammunition pouch and waistbelt. The gas mask was carried in a canvas bag on the left hip.

Weapons: Russian Moisin M.1891–30 7·62 mm. rifle. The bayonet was normally carried on the rifle, either in a fixed or 'reversed' position, when not actually in use, but in this particular case the soldier wears a leather scabbard.

48 U.S.S.R.: Captain Internal Security Troops (N.K.V.D.), 1941

Internal Security Troops were organised along military lines with their own armour and artillery. N.K.V.D. personnel wore army uniform with their own distinguishing colours – strawberry and light blue – which appeared on the cap and collar patches and later on the shoulder boards.

Equipment: Regulation officer's waistbelt.

49 Great Britain: Brigadier New-Biggin, Chief Administration officer, Singapore 1942

The khaki drill shirt and shorts were the normal everyday wear for British troops in the tropics. Officers also had a lightweight service dress consisting of single-breasted tunic and long trousers.

Equipment: Regulation officer's 'Sam Browne' belt.

50 The Netherlands: Private, Royal Dutch Indian Legion, Dutch East indies, 1942

The lightweight version of the grey-green field service uniform was worn in the tropics by both soldiers and marines.

Equipment: Knil-model equipment with gas mask on the chest.

Weapons: Dutch 6·5 mm. Hembrug M.1895 rifle.

51 India: Lieutenant 19th Hyderabad Regiment, Singapore, February 1942

Again the K.D. shirt and shorts with khaki stockings and short puttees forming the basic field service order for English officers in Indian infantry regiments.

Equipment: Pattern 1937 web equipment, basic set for officers with map case.

Weapons: British Webley ·455 Mark VI Pistol No. 1.

49 *British officer*   50 *Dutch infantryman*   51 *Indian infantry officer*

52 *French general*   53 *British general*   54 *British staff officer*

52 France: Brigadier Philipe de Haute-Clocque (better known as Leclerc), Commander L. Force, North Africa 1942
Leclerc wears a *pelisse coloniale*, which was very popular with French colonial officers. The anchor badge on the collar was common to all French colonial troops.

53 Great Britain: General Sir Bernard Law Montgomery K.C.B., D.S.O., Commander British 8th Army, North Africa 1942
Monty's individual style of dress had nothing to do with regulations and makes an interesting comparison with the rather more martial-looking Wavell and Rommel.

54 Great Britain: Captain, North Africa 1942
This staff officer wears the K.D. shirt and shorts with long woollen stockings and his service dress peaked cap. His rank badges are attached to a detachable slide on the shoulder straps.

Equipment: Pattern 1937 web equipment set for personnel armed with pistol only.

Weapons: British Webley ·455 Mark VI pistol No. 1.

55 Germany: Lieutenant-Colonel 33rd Engineer Battalion 15th Armoured Division, North Africa 1942
The steel helmet, although heavy and hot and in short supply, was usually worn in action, and any available goggles were used to protect the eyes from sun and sand.

Equipment: Officer' waistbelt, folding entrenching tool and binoculars.

56 Germany: Colonel-General Erwin Rommel, Commander Panzer Army Africa, North Africa 1942
Rommel's eccentricities of dress were not as extreme as Monty's, and were limited to a tartan scarf and British anti-gas goggles, which he wore on his cap. Many German officers wore bits and pieces of their temperate uniform in the desert, as did the Allies.

Equipment: 10 × 50 service binoculars.

57 Germany: Acting corporal 200th Panzer Grenadier Regiment (15th Pz. Div.), North Africa 1942
The greatcoat was very necessary in the bitter cold nights, and apart from the olive-green pullover and socks, it was the only woollen item of tropical clothing. The two grenadier regiments of the 15th Pz. Div. identified themselves by a strip of red or green cloth across the shoulder strap.

Equipment: Web waistbelt and straps supporting, brown leather ammunition pouches and water bottle on the right hip.

Weapons: German Mauser Gew. 98k service rifle.

55 *German engineer officer*   56 *German general*   57 *German infantryman*

58 *German infantry officer*   59 *German infantryman*   60 *Italian mountain troop officer*

58 Germany: Captain of infantry, Cholm 1942
Typical of improvised winter uniforms during the first Russian winter of the war were the white-washed helmet and one or more greatcoats over which some kind of white cotton smock or sheet was worn as camouflage. The boots are Russian fel *valenki*.

Equipment: Other ranks' waistbelt and dispatch case, with MP 38 or 40 magazine pouches and infantry straps supporting.

59 Germany: Private 386th Infantry Regiment, Russia 1942
Standard field-grey field service uniform with matching trousers.

Equipment: The battle pack was made up of a webbing frame to which were strapped an iron ration pack, groundsheet and mess-tin, with a greatcoat strapped on the outside. On the left hip is carried the entrenching tool and bayonet. The gas mask is suspended over the right shoulder by a webbing strap, and on the right hip is the canvas haversack.

Weapons: German Mauser 98k rifle.

60 Italy: Lieutenant-Colonel 8th Alpine Regiment 3rd Julia Alpine Division, Russia 1942
Mountain troops wore the felt hat with a different feather according to rank. The greatcoat and trousers are the special winter model introduced for use on the eastern front.

Equipment: Service binoculars.

61 U.S.A.: Major-General A.M. Patch, Commander U.S. force, Guadalcanl 1942–3

Patch wears the basic khaki drill tropical uniform of the U.S. army with his service dress peaked cap.

Equipment: Basic webbing belt and leather automatic pistol holster.

Weapons: U.S. ·45 1911 or 1911A1 automatic pistol.

62 U.S.A.: Private 23rd Infantry Division, Guadalcanal 1942–3

The one-piece olive-drab herringbone-twill overall was originally intended for fatigues, but was found to be the most practical stop-gap combat dress available at the beginning of the war.

Equipment: Standard woven waistbelt with ammunition pouches and cotton bandoliers for additional ammunition.

Weapons: 1903 Springfield.

63 Australia: Infantryman 17th Australian Brigade, Wau New Guinea 1942

This basically British uniform with the Australian 'wide awake' hat was later in the war to become the most popular form of head-dress in the far east.

Equipment: Pattern 1937 web equipment with gas mask (rarely worn in the jungle,) enamel cup and small pack.

Weapons: British rifle No. 1 SMLE Mark III.

61 *US general*   62 *US infantryman*   63 *Australian infantryman*

64 *Chinese infantryman*   65 *Chinese general*   66 *Chinese infantryman*

64 China: Private Nationalist infantry, China 1939

Germany has been responsible for the training of the Chinese army, which accounts for the rather Germanic appearance of this infantryman.

Equipment: Normally made of natural-coloured leather, although much was made from canvas. The pack usually consisted of a canvas bundle with bedding roll strapped on three sides, metal mess tin and a cloth tube containing rice, which was either tied to the pack or worn over the shoulder or round the neck.

Weapons: German or Chinese-made Mauser 7 mm. rifles or other types imported from all over the world.

65 China: Generalissimo Chiang Kai Shek, China 1941

This was the regulation officer's service dress throughout the war, although it was made in many variations and different colours and types of clothing according to local conditions.

Equipment: Brown leather officer's waist-belt and cross-strap.

66 China: Private Communist infantry, Shensi Province China 1938

In winter both communists and nationalists wore grey or blue cotton wadded uniforms, while badges of rank remained the same on both sides. In place of the nationalist sun emblem, communists used the five-pointed red star.

Equipment: Ammunition was carried in cloth cartridge bandoliers.

Weapons: Communist forces received weapons from Russia or used captured Japanese ones.

67 Japan: Lieutenant tank troops, China 1938
This officer wears the old-style M.90 other ranks' greatcoat over a woollen pullover. The tank helmet was made of brown canvas and was designed to protect the head from inside the vehicle.

Equipment: Regulation officer's waistbelt and cross-strap, with pistol holster suspended from a strap over the left shoulder.

Weapons: Japanese nambu Type 1904 8 mm. automatic pistol and sword (not showing).

68 Japan: Major, Mukden 1938
This is the standard M.98 (1938) Japanese officer' service dress with the duty officer's sash.

Weapons: Regulation officer's sword in the *Seki* style.

69 Japan: Private of infantry, Manchuria 1938
The old-style sleeveless winter coat was made of cotton or sometimes sheepskin.

Equipment: Standard infantry belt and ammunition pouches.

67 *Japanese tank officer*   68 *Japanese staff officer*   69 *Japanese infantryman*

70 *French infantryman* 71 *British infantryman* 72 *US tank man*

70 France: Private colonial infantry, Tunisia 1943

The steel helmet bears the anchor badge of French colonial infantry. The rest of the uniform consists of the 1940-pattern British battle dress with exposed buttons.

Equipment: British-pattern 1937 web equipment.

Weapons: British rifle No. 1 Mark III.

71 Great Britain: Private Queen's Royal Regiment (8th Army), Tunis May 1943

The cap G.S., although similar in shape to a beret, was not as popular, due to its stiffness. The rest of the uniform is standard British khaki drill tropical dress.

Equipment: Pattern 1937 web equipment with binocular case on the left hip.

Weapons: British rifle No. 1 Mark III.

72 U.S.A.: Sergeant (Grade 4) Armoured Forces, Tunisia 1943

The composition helmet was intended as a lightweight protection for the head from possible injury inside the tank. The zip-fronted field jacket has the early style of pockets, which were later replaced by vertical slash pockets.

Equipment: Basic web belt and cartridge case and brown leather pistol holder.

Weapons: U.S. ·45 1911A1 (Colt 45) automatic pistol.

73 Germany: Captain 334th Artillery Regiment, Tunis May 1943
This is basically the olive-green tropical field service dress which had been worn in North Africa since the German arrival. By the end of the campaign the steel helmet had completely replaced the sun helmet.

Equipment: Regulation officer's waistbelt and standard issue dispatch case.

74 Germany: Mayor von Meyer, A.D.C. to General Cramer, last Commander of the German African Corps, May 1943
Major von Meyer wears the traditional cap badge which was worn by regimental staff and 2nd and 4th Squdrons of the 6th Cavalry Regiment, and by the 3rd Motorcycle Battalion. He also wears the black armoured troop tie.

Equipment: Regulation officer's waistbelt.

75 Italy: Marshal of Italy Ettore Bastico, C-in-C. Axis Forces in North Africa, 1943
Bastico wears the leather armoured vehicle crew coat over standard officer's tropical uniform.

73 *German artillery officer*   74 *German cavalry officer*   75 *Italian general*

76 *Italian paratrooper*   77 *German mountain troop officer*   78 *German paratrooper*

76 Italy: Private II battalion 184th Parachute Regiment, Nembo
Although German-influenced, this uniform was of Italian manufacture. The parachute badge on the left breast is that of the Libyan Parachute Battalion which was disbanded in 1941.

Equipment: German air-force waistbelt and buckle.

Weapons: German stick grenade 24 and egg grenade 39, and Italian MVSN (Black-Shirt) dagger.

77 Germany: 2nd lieutenant mountain rifle regiment, Italy 1943
Contrary to popular belief tropical clothing was worn by German troops not only in Africa, but in all tropical and sub-tropical countries.

Equipment: Regulation officer's waistbelt.

78 Germany: Corporal 1st Company Parachute Demonstration Battalion, Gran Sasso September 1943
The paratroop smock, known as the 'bone sack', was made in a number of different colours and versions – olive-green with and without pockets, light khaki for tropical use, and later in geometric, and finally blurred, camouflage patterns. All pockets and openings were closed with with zip-fasteners or press-studs. The side cap and trousers were part of the standard air-force tropical clothing.

Equipment: Regulation brown leather air-force other ranks' belt and buckle, straps supporting and entrenching tool.

Weapons: German paratroop rifle (*Fallschirmgewehr* – FG-42) 7·92 mm. automatic rifle.

79 Denmark: Member of the Danish Resistance Movement, 1945
As long as resisters had to blend with the civilian population they could not wear uniform, and it was only for a very short period between the German capitulation and the Allied arrival that members of the resistance donned helmets and armlets.

Weapons: Swedish Model 37–99 9 mm. submachine gun.

80 France: Franc-Tireur French Forces of the Interior (F.F.I.), France 1944
In the more remote regions of France resistance groups became full-time partisan units while some adopted the Cross of Lorraine as their emblem.

Weapons: British Bren ·303 Light machine-gun.

81 Italy: Communist partisan of the 47th Garibaldi Brigade, Parma Apennines, 1944
Communist partisans were well organised along military lines with their own system of rank badges (red stars and horizontal bars) which were worn on the left breast.

Equipment: Submachine-gun magazines were carried either in the pocket or in pouches made of canvas or leather.

Weapons: British Sten Mark II submachine-gun and British mills hand grenade.

79 *Danish resistance man*   80 *French resistance man*   81 *Italian partisan*

82 *Australian infantryman*   83 *US tank man*   84 *US marauder*

82 Australia: Commando 8th Australian Infantry Battalion, Solomon Islands 1944
By this stage in the war Australian uniform in the Far East included much American clothing such as the trousers and gaiters.

Equipment: Pattern 1937 web equipment, although U.S. equipment was also widely used.

Weapons: Australian ·303 rifle No. 1 Mark III.

83 U.S.A.: Staff Sergeant (Grade 3) Armoured forces, Solomon Islands 1943
In the Far East the most common tank outfit was the one-piece herringbone twill overall, and the lightweight fibre helmet.

Equipment: Standard woven belt with leather pistol holster.

Weapons: U.S. ·45 M.1928 A1 Thompson submachine-gun.

84 U.S.A.: Merrill's Marauders, Northern Burma March 1944
The U.S. answer to Wingate's Chindits was the 530th Composite Unit (Prov.), better known under its more romantic name of Merrill's Marauders. Every soldier found by a process of elimination his ideal combat *dress*.

Equipment: Standard woven belt, ammunition pouches and water bottle.

Weapons: U.S. M.1 carbine and M.4 knife bayonet, and native *kukri*.

85 Germany: Private People's Grenadier Regiment, Germany 1945

Volksgrenadier personnel did not wear any distinctive uniform or insignia, but because they were formed at the end of the war their uniforms tended to be of the final standard pattern.

Equipment: Standard infantry equipment with blanket strapped to the pack, and water bottle with plastic cup.

Weapons: German Mauser 98k rifle of late manufacture with laminated wooden stock. On his shoulder he carries a disposable anti-tank projectile (Panzerfaust 60).

86 Germany: Leader of the NSDAP, Reich Chancellor, and Commander-in-Chief of the German Armed Forces, Adolf Hitler, Berlin April 1945

Hitler's wartime uniform mirrored his dual position as political leader and military commander, and combined features of NSDAP and army uniform.

87 Germany: Home Guardsman (Volks-sturmmann), Germany 1945

Instituted in 1944, the German Home Guard called upon every able-bodied male between the ages of 16 and 60. There was no uniform as such but all existing military, para-military and party uniforms were worn in conjunction with an armbelt bearing the inscription 'Deutsche Volkssturm Wehrmacht' (German Armed Forces Home Guard).

Equipment: Whatever was available.

Weapons: Austrian Mannlicher M.188 8 mm. rifle.

85 *German people's grenadier*   86 *German leader*   87 *German home guardsman*

88 *Russian infantryman*   89 *Russian marshal*   90 *Russian infantry officer*

88 U.S.R.: Private of infantry, Moscow 1945
Full-dress uniform was introduced in January 1943, and was worn with a peaked cap as a walking-out dress. The standard is that of Adolf Hitler's Bodyguard Regiment which was captured by the Russians in Berlin.

89 U.S.S.R.: Marshal of the Soviet Union M. Malinovsky, Moscow 1945
The sea-green (the colour was formerly known as Tsar's green), full-dress uniform for marshals and generals was introduced in 1945, specially for the victory celebrations and parades. The uniform included many pre-1914 Imperial Russian uniform features.

Weapons: Soviet version of the last pattern Tsarist officer's sabre.

90 U.S.S.R.: Lieutenant of infantry, Berlin 1945
The officer's full-dress tunic was basically identical with the other rank's version, except that field officers had two spools on the cuffs and two gold lace bars on the collar patches, whereas company officers had only one.

Equipment: Regulation M.1935 officer's waistbelt and buckle.